P9-CFF-690

What Makes Me A
JEHOVAH'S
WITNESS?

Marie Juettner

KIDHAVEN PRESS

An imprint of Thomson Gale, a part of The Thomson Corporation

THOMSON

*

™

© 2006 Thomson Gale, a part of The Thomson Corporation.

Thomson and Star Logo are trademarks and Gale and KidHaven Press are registered trademarks used herein under license.

For more information, contact
KidHaven Press
27500 Drake Rd.
Farmington Hills, MI 48331-3535
Or you can visit our Internet site at http://www.gale.com

LIBRARY OF CONGRESS CATALOGING-IN-PUBLICATION DATA

Juettner, Marie.
  Jehovah's Witness / by Marie Juettner.
    p. cm. — (What Makes Me a— ?)
  Includes bibliographical references and index.
  ISBN 0-7377-3084-6 (hardcover)
  1. Jehovah's Witnesses—Juvenile literature. I. Title. II. Series.
BX8526.J84 2005
289.9'2—dc22
                                                      2005024321

Printed in the United States of America

CONTENTS

INTRODUCTION

Old and New

Jehovah's Witnesses are a recently formed **denomination**, or branch, of an old religion, Christianity. While Christianity has existed for more than 2,000 years, the Jehovah's Witness sect was not founded until the late 1800s.

The United States, the country where Jehovah's Witnesses were founded, has the greatest concentration of Witnesses anywhere in the world—1.5 million. However, Jehovah's Witnesses live on every continent except Antarctica. There are 6.5 million Witnesses around the world. The *Watchtower*, a magazine published by Jehovah's Witnesses, is published in 400 languages. Watch Tower videos are produced in nineteen different languages. Currently, Jehovah's Witnesses are expanding the fastest in Latin America.

Like other Christians, Jehovah's Witnesses revere the *Bible* as their holy scripture. (They have their own trans-

A few of the world's more than 6.5 million Jehovah's Witnesses take part in an outdoor prayer session in Spain.

lation of the *Bible,* the New World Translation.) Witnesses base the name of their religion on a verse from the *Bible, Isaiah* 43:12, which states, "Ye are my witnesses, saith Jehovah, and I am God." The word ***witness*** means a person who can report about something based on his or her own experience. For example, a person who provides evidence to a court of law by telling about something he or she saw is a witness. However, a witness can also be a person who testifies about his or her religious faith. Jehovah's Witnesses consider themselves witnesses in both senses of the word. They believe that they have experienced God's actions in their own lives, and they want to tell others about their experience. Sharing their faith with others is part of their religious practice.

CHAPTER ONE

How Did My Religion Begin?

C hristianity began more than 2,000 years ago, with the death of Jesus of Nazareth. Jehovah's Witnesses are a denomination, or branch, of Christianity. Jehovah's Witnesses share much of their history, especially the lives of Jesus and his disciples, with other Christians. But Witnesses also have their own history, beginning with their founder, Charles Taze Russell.

Charles Taze Russell

Charles Taze Russell, the founder of Jehovah's Witnesses, was born in 1852 in Allegheny, Pennsylvania. He grew up as a Presbyterian but later joined the Congregationalist Church. Although devoted to Christianity, Russell grew troubled by one belief of his church. As a Presbyterian, he was taught that God condemned evil people and non-Christians to eternal damnation in hell. Russell did not think that a loving God would condemn anyone to hell. For a year, this troubled him so much that he gave up religion altogether. Then he renewed his belief in Christianity. Russell eventually came to believe that hell is a metaphor for total destruction and that "going to hell" simply means dying, never to be resurrected.

Like all Christians, Jehovah's Witnesses follow the teachings of Jesus Christ, shown in this painting after he was crucified.

In the 1870s, Charles Taze Russell grew dissatisfied with the teachings of existing Christian churches and he decided to establish a new church.

Not satisfied with any of the Christian churches he visited, Russell decided to form his own *Bible* study group. At that time, Russell's followers were simply called Russellites, and their organization was known as the Bible Students Association. One of Russell's primary beliefs was that the world would end soon and that the kingdom of God would begin.

Russell had calculated the date he thought would mark the beginning of the kingdom of God on Earth. He preached that Jesus had returned to Earth in 1874 but that his return had taken place invisibly. Russell thought that since 1874, Jesus had been present on Earth in spirit. He predicted that on October 2, 1914, the world's governments would fall and Jesus would begin to rule the Earth as its king. That day, all those who had died would have the opportunity to accept God or to return to death forever. This would be the end of the world as humanity had known it, an end time that Christians call **Armageddon**. Before that happened, though, Russell claimed that certain "living saints," including himself and his followers, would be taken bodily into heaven to live with God. He believed he knew the date this would occur: Good Friday, April 1878.

Pennsylvania newspapers reported that on that night, Russell and his followers donned white robes, went to Pittsburgh's Sixth Street Bridge, and waited there to be carried into heaven. Russell later denied it. The one thing historians are certain of, though, is that no Russellites were carried away into heaven that night. Russell remained on Earth and continued his preaching. Jehovah's Witnesses now consider the 1878 date to have been a miscalculation.

Russell was disappointed by his miscalculation, but he did not lose his faith. He and his followers began publishing a pamphlet called *Zion's Watchtower and Herald of Christ's Presence*. The pamphlet explained Russell's views about Jesus's return. In 1881, the group formed the Zion's Watch Tower Tract Society. Later, the name was changed to Watch Tower Bible and Tract Society.

In this medieval woodcut, the good are led to Jesus's side while the wicked are punished by demons as the world comes to an end.

By 1888, the Watch Tower Society had 50 full-time employees going door-to-door with pamphlets and tracts. (A tract is a small booklet that advocates a particular point of view.)

The door-to-door method of converting people proved to be quite successful. The Witnesses estimate that in 1890, Russell had 400 followers. By October 1, 1914, the Russellites had grown to 50,000 members, all of whom expected God's kingdom on Earth to be established the next day. When this did not occur, thousands of Russellites left the church. Russell again gave a reason for God's absence. He began preaching that although the date for Armageddon had arrived, God had decided to show mercy to humanity. He said that Jesus had become king of heaven and that Satan had been exiled from heaven to live on Earth. Satan's arrival on Earth was the reason for the outbreak of World War

Christian Populations of the World

Roman Catholics	1,076,951,000
Protestants	349,792,000
Orthodox	217,522,000
Anglicans	81,663,000
Jehovah's Witnesses	**6,513,000**
Independents	398,085,000

I, Russell claimed. But instead of sending Jesus immediately to take charge of Earth, God had chosen to provide more time for humans to learn about his coming kingdom. Russell then wrote, "Even if the time of our change should not come within ten years, what more should we ask? Are we not a blessed, happy people? Is not our God faithful? If anyone knows anything better, let him take it."[1]

Russell also admitted that he could have made a mistake in calculating the exact date for Armageddon. Calculating such a date, his followers pointed out, was a complicated matter. Russell, and later the Jehovah's Witnesses, calculate the dates when they expect Armageddon to occur by referring to predictions in the *Bible*. Predicting the date of Armageddon remains important to Jehovah's Witnesses today.

Name Change

Russell died in 1916, and Joseph Rutherford was elected leader of the Watch Tower group. Under his leadership, the group took the name Jehovah's Witnesses in 1931. And they continued to prophesy the date for Armageddon. First they predicted 1918, then 1920, then 1925, then 1941, and finally 1975. None of these dates proved to be accurate. But Witnesses remain convinced that Armageddon is fast approaching. They expect the history of their religion, and all religions, to come to an end very soon.

CHAPTER TWO

What Do I Believe?

Jehovah's Witnesses believe many of the same things that other Christians believe. They consider the *Bible* to be the word of God. They revere Jesus as God's only son. But Jehovah's Witnesses differ from other Christians in some ways.

Jesus and Jehovah

Most Christians believe in a three-in-one God called the Trinity. The Trinity consists of God, Jesus, and the Holy Spirit. Christians believe that all three members of the Trinity are aspects of the one God. In other words, they believe that God is God, Jesus is God, and the Holy Spirit is God.

Jehovah's Witnesses, although they believe in the Christian God, do not consider Jesus to be God, nor do they see him as God's equal. Witnesses do believe, as other Christians do, that Jesus is God's son and that he

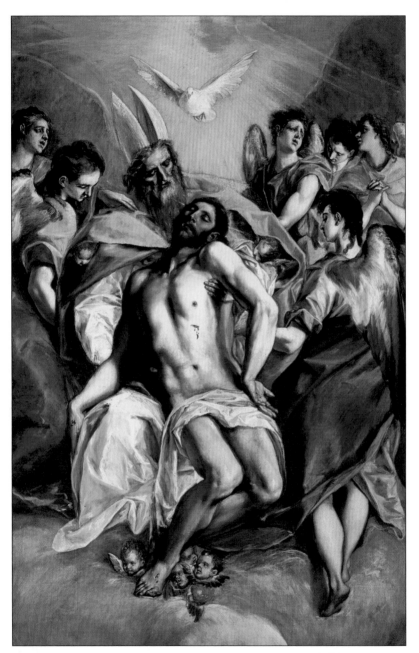

Jehovah's Witnesses do not believe in the Holy Trinity of God the
Father (background), Jesus the Son (center), and the Holy Spirit,
seen in this painting as a dove.

died in place of the rest of humanity to save humans from their sins. Witnesses do not believe, however, that simply accepting Jesus's sacrifice is enough to make a person a member of God's kingdom forever. Rather, they believe that one must first accept Jesus, and then continue to obey God.

Jesus is very important to Jehovah's Witnesses, however. Witnesses expect Jesus to rule the **kingdom of God** on Earth. Under Jesus's rule, they believe, no one will be oppressed. Instead, there will be peace forever. Witnesses believe that Jesus's rule will begin very soon, within the lifetimes of some people who are alive today. First, however, God's Armageddon will destroy all evil on Earth.

Heaven and Hell

Jehovah's Witnesses do not believe, as many Christians do, in an afterlife in which people go to heaven if they have accepted Jesus or to hell if they have not. Instead, they believe that when Jesus comes to Earth to rule the kingdom of God, God's kingdom will include all people, those currently living and those who have previously died. Dead people will be **resurrected**, or restored to life, both in their body and their soul. Dead people who were not Christians when they died will have a chance to become Christians. People who do not become Christians will simply die and cease to exist. They will not go to hell.

Jehovah's Witnesses do believe in heaven, however. They believe that when Jesus begins ruling the kingdom of God, he will live not on Earth, but in heaven, along with 144,000 "true Christians." Everyone else will live in the kingdom of God on Earth. If they obey God, they will live forever in peace and harmony.

The End Times

Jehovah's Witnesses believe the kingdom of God will begin on Earth very soon. Witnesses believe that we are living in the **end times**, the time when the war of Armageddon will begin. They believe that Jesus began ruling heaven in 1914. When Jesus begins to rule Earth, Witnesses believe, all existing governments will fall. At that point, all those who have already died will be resurrected and have the opportunity to accept God or choose to remain dead forever.

Jehovah's Witnesses believe the news that Jesus will soon rule the world is urgent, which is why they go door-to-door telling people about it. In the early years after the founding of the Jehovah's Witness sect, some Witnesses believed strongly that the kingdom of God would come very soon, perhaps the next day or next week. They kept guest rooms ready in their homes for the arrival of previously dead relatives and postponed medical treatment that would become unnecessary once the kingdom of God began. They even delayed marriage, believing that it was foolish to have children if the war of Armageddon was about to begin. Today, Jehovah's Witnesses still expect the kingdom of God to begin soon, but they no longer delay medical treatment or marriage based on that expectation.

In this painting, Jesus passes judgment on all humankind to determine who shall live for all eternity at his side.

Family Life

Like most Christians, Jehovah's Witnesses have strong beliefs about the importance of marriage and the family. Witnesses do not date unless they are considering marriage. Once they do marry, Jehovah's Witnesses view husbands and wives as partners, working together to take care of the family. However, Witnesses also believe that men should be the heads of their households and that women should support them in that role. When couples disagree, Witnesses believe the wife should submit to the authority of the husband. Couples who have strong differences of opinion should seek counseling, rather than get divorced. However, in extreme situations, Jehovah's Witnesses do get divorced. For example, the founder of Jehovah's Witnesses, Charles Taze Russell, divorced his wife for failing to obey him. Jehovah's Witnesses also allow divorce when a husband or wife has formed a relationship with another person or has become violent.

Citizenship

Jehovah's Witnesses try to be peaceful, law-abiding citizens of the countries in which they live. However, because they believe that all current governments will soon fall and that they can only be true citizens of the kingdom of God, Jehovah's Witnesses will not do certain things. They refuse to swear allegiance to any nation, sing the national anthem of the country in which they live, or salute its flag. They also

Jehovah's Witnesses do not serve in the military nor salute a flag, but do not try to prevent others from doing so.

refuse to serve in any nation's military forces. Witnesses living in democratic countries do not vote or run for public office. They consider these practices to be **idolatry**, or worshipping a false god. Only the true God, Jehovah, they believe, can command the loyalty and allegiance of followers.

Jehovah's Witnesses do not try to prevent other people from serving in the military, voting, or saluting the flag. They consider themselves neutral with respect to politics and wars. However, throughout their history, Witnesses have frequently been persecuted because of their beliefs about citizenship. During World War II, persecution of Witnesses turned violent. In the United States, many Witnesses were kidnapped, beaten, and tarred and feathered because they refused to salute the flag. (At first, American children of Jehovah's Witnesses were sometimes expelled from school for refusing to salute the flag, but later the Supreme Court ruled that children could not be forced to salute the flag in school.) Male Witnesses were jailed for refusing to serve in the military after being drafted. In Nazi Germany, Jehovah's Witnesses also refused to serve in the military or salute the flag. They were sent to concentration camps, where approximately 2,000 Witnesses died.

Health

Although Jehovah's Witnesses have been heavily criticized for their beliefs about citizenship, they have probably been most criticized for their beliefs about blood transfusions. When a patient loses so much blood that his or her life is in danger, doctors can transfuse donated blood from another person into the patient's veins.

A Difficult Choice

Blood transfusions save the lives of many seriously ill or injured patients who would otherwise die. Witnesses, though, believe that it is against God's law to ingest, or eat, blood, even if the blood is taken into one's body through the veins. They believe that Christians should obey the exact words of God, as found in the *Bible*. They point to verses such as *Leviticus* 17:10–11, which reads: "If anyone of the house of Israel or of the strangers who reside among them partakes of any blood, I will set My face against the person who partakes of the blood, and I will cut him off from among his kin. For the life of the flesh is in the blood."[2] Witnesses interpret verses like this one as meaning not only that they may not eat foods that contain blood, but also that they may not receive blood transfusions or transplanted organs from organ donors. For this reason, Jehovah's Witnesses who need surgery, or whose children need surgery, sometimes face a difficult choice. They **pray** about the decision first. Then they usually choose to instruct their doctors to do everything possible to help them survive surgery but not to give them a blood transfusion even if it seems medically necessary to do so. This means that sometimes Witnesses and children of Witnesses die when a blood transfusion could have saved them. Other times doctors are able to save them without using a blood transfusion. Witnesses

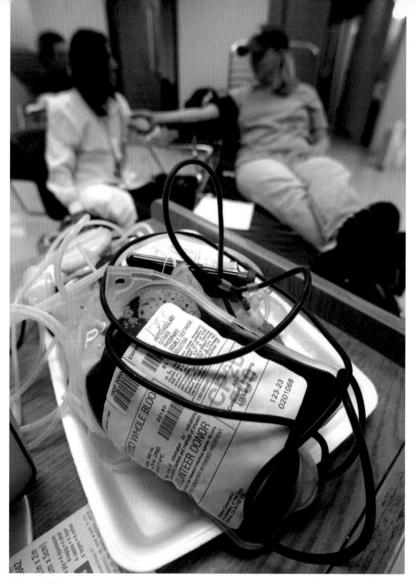

Many Witnesses will not accept blood transfusions, believing it goes against God's will to ingest blood, even through the veins.

believe that they can survive without a blood transfusion if it is God's will for them to do so.

Jehovah's Witnesses tend to live healthfully, and most never have to make the difficult choice about whether or not to receive a blood transfusion. They practice preventive medicine whenever possible, eating

Regular exercise is an important part of the healthy lifestyle Witnesses lead.

nutritious food and exercising regularly. Witnesses also try to prevent health problems by not ingesting harmful substances. For example, they do not smoke, and they avoid drinking alcohol and taking any medication.

When Jehovah's Witnesses face an ethical dilemma, they try to solve it by studying the *Bible* and by praying. They study the *Bible* because they consider it to be the true word of God about many subjects, and when they pray, they pray only to God, not to Jesus or to any saints. The most fundamental belief of Jehovah's Witnesses is that they should obey the will of God. Their belief that they are acting out God's will gives Witnesses the courage to continue practicing their faith even when some members of the community exclude or attack them.

CHAPTER THREE

How Do I Practice My Faith?

Like other Christians, Jehovah's Witnesses practice their faith by being **baptized**, going to church, praying, and trying to lead good and moral lives. Jehovah's Witnesses also feel a duty to go door-to-door telling people about the kingdom of God.

Baptism

When people decide to **convert**, or change their religion, and become Jehovah's Witnesses, they must go through a special period of time in which church elders make sure that they understand the faith. Because children and babies may not understand all the beliefs of Jehovah's Witnesses, church elders never agree to baptize anyone who is not an adult. Elders also try to make sure that believers are choosing to convert voluntarily, which means that no one is forcing them to convert. When elders are sure of this, believers can be baptized.

A church elder baptizes an adult woman who has chosen to become a Jehovah's Witness.

Jehovah's Witnesses baptize new converts by completely immersing them in water. Jehovah's Witnesses, like most Christians, consider baptism to be a kind of second birth. It is the beginning of a new life as a member of their faith.

Going to Church

Jehovah's Witnesses call their churches kingdom halls. They want people to know that the act of gathering together to worship God is more important than the place where they gather. For this reason, kingdom halls are very plain and simple. Most have been built by volunteer Witnesses themselves.

Like other Christian churches, Jehovah's Witnesses open their church services to anyone who wants to attend. They do not collect an offering, but they encourage members of the church to donate privately.

All adult Jehovah's Witnesses, both men and women, are ministers of their church. They train to be ministers by taking classes at church. (Children can take classes too, but they are not baptized until they are old enough to understand the choice to become a Witness.) Jehovah's Witnesses do not attend the special schools, called seminaries, where most other Christian ministers receive their training. Although all members of the

Volunteer Witnesses in Detroit help to build a new church, known as a kingdom hall.

church are ministers, only the elders of the congregation, called congregation servants, lead the services.

Many denominations of Christianity expect members to attend a weekly church service on Sunday. Jehovah's Witnesses, however, meet five times a week. On Sunday, they hear a public talk. This is usually an hourlong sermon on a topic from the *Bible*. After the talk (or at another time), Witnesses meet again to discuss an article from the *Watchtower* magazine, the official magazine of Jehovah's Witnesses.

One weekday evening, Jehovah's Witnesses attend ministry school, called Theocratic Ministry School. During ministry school meetings, several students give

A large group of Witnesses prays during one of the five meetings they have each week.

speeches on topics from the *Bible*, and a teacher gives the students constructive feedback. Once a week, after ministry school, Witnesses meet to train for various ministry activities. Sometimes elders talk at these meetings about issues that the congregation is currently concerned about. But most of the time, members spend this time preparing for door-to-door witnessing.

On another weekday evening, or on Saturday, Jehovah's Witnesses meet in small groups to study a *Bible* topic. They read a *Watchtower* magazine article or brochure, ask each other questions based on it, and answer the questions using their knowledge of the *Bible*. For these meetings, Witnesses often gather in each other's homes, rather than in a kingdom hall. Sometimes Witnesses also meet at a kingdom hall, however, for additional *Bible* study classes and for social gatherings.

Prayer

Like all Christians, Jehovah's Witnesses pray by talking to God. They pray as part of the service at the kingdom hall on Sundays, but they also pray individually, as part of everyday life. Frequently, they pray for guidance in understanding the *Bible*. Understanding the *Bible* is important to Witnesses, because they use it as a guide for moral conduct. Witnesses also pray on behalf of members who are ill or who are going through a personal crisis. Jehovah's Witnesses do not expect God to grant all of their requests. They believe that God knows better than they do what is best for them. But they do believe that God answers prayers.

Holidays

Jehovah's Witnesses do not celebrate birthdays or most holidays. For example, they do not celebrate Thanksgiving, Christmas, or Easter. They believe that the practice of celebrating these holidays dates back to ancient pagan religions and that the early Christians did not celebrate holidays. Jehovah's Witnesses do celebrate one holiday, however. They celebrate the anniversary of Jesus's death. Witnesses remember this event by meeting together for a meal of bread and wine on Maundy Thursday, the day before Good Friday. They do this in memory of the Last Supper, the meal that Jesus ate with his disciples on the Thursday before his execution.

Witnessing

Witnessing is the most well-known practice of Jehovah's Witnesses. All members are expected to volunteer some time going door-to-door, talking with people about their faith. Witnesses believe that they have an urgent duty to let people know that soon the kingdom of God will begin and they will be able to live in peace and harmony forever. Because they consider this news so urgent, Witnesses try to go door-to-door at least once a week. Children are encouraged to witness along with their parents. While witnessing, Jehovah's Witnesses offer literature, including the *Watchtower* magazine, to anyone who is interested. (They give the *Watchtower* magazine and pamphlets away freely; they never sell them.)

Two Jehovah's Witnesses in New York read aloud from the *Bible* in a public place as they try to interest others in their faith.

In addition to going door-to-door, Witnesses are expected to witness informally to the people they interact with socially. When they talk to coworkers or to friends who are not Jehovah's Witnesses, they try to find opportunities to tell them about their faith.

Clean Living

Jehovah's Witnesses believe that they must act as Witnesses not only at church and while praying and witnessing, but also during their everyday lives. They advocate what some people call clean living. This means that they try to eat healthfully; avoid tobacco, drugs, and alcohol; and obey the laws of their society whenever possible.

A Jehovah's Witness passes out copies of the church's magazine, *Watchtower*, in New York City.

In each Jehovah's Witness congregation there is a group of elders, who are respected older members of the church. The elders encourage the members of the community to maintain high moral standards. If a member of the community behaves in a way that Witnesses consider immoral, the elders talk informally with the member or encourage others, such as family members, to talk with the member about his or her activities. In very rare cases, a Jehovah's Witness is asked to leave his or her congregation if he or she refuses to follow the church's moral guidelines. This practice is called **disfellowshipping**.

As Jehovah's Witnesses decide how to practice their faith, they use one principle to help them decide what to do. They try to follow the guidance of Jehovah (God). When in doubt, Witnesses turn to the *Bible,* which they believe contains Jehovah's exact words and instructions. Because they do their best to obey God at all times, Witnesses feel certain they are living good and moral lives.

CHAPTER FOUR

What Challenges Does My Religion Face Today?

Jehovah's Witnesses try to obey the laws and to be good citizens of the countries in which they live. Some countries, however, have laws that make it challenging to be both a Jehovah's Witness and a good citizen.

A License to Pray

Many countries have state religions, religions that are endorsed by the government. Some countries have just one state religion. For example, in Saudi Arabia, the state religion is Islam. In Armenia, the Armenian Apostolic Church, a denomination of Christianity, is the state religion. The state religion of most Communist countries is atheism. In some countries, practicing a religion other than the official state religion is against the law. In these countries, Jehovah's Witnesses can be arrested and jailed simply for practicing their faith. In many other countries, such as Singapore and Uzbekistan, the government allows people to practice a few other religions, but requires those religions to be licensed by the government. Jehovah's Witnesses frequently cannot obtain a license to practice their religion.

Human Rights Abuses

What happens to Jehovah's Witnesses who live in countries where their religion is illegal? Often, police raid meetings of Jehovah's Witnesses, even when the meetings take place in private homes. They arrest the Witnesses at the

In 2004 a group of Witnesses listens as a judge in Moscow delivers a ruling that prevents them from openly practicing their religion in the Russian capital.

meeting and sometimes beat them. In Uzbekistan, police raid the Witnesses' celebration of Maundy Thursday every year. They question Witnesses, search them, charge them fines, take away their passports, arrest them, and beat them.

In Turkmenistan, where Jehovah's Witness meetings are often raided, women often must take babies and children to jail with them or are forced to leave their children behind without anyone to care for them. In the country of Georgia, Jehovah's Witnesses and other Christians who are not Eastern Orthodox are sometimes attacked, not only by police but by gangs of civilians. These gangs stalk non-Orthodox Christians on the way to and from prayer meetings. They break into homes, destroy property, burn religious books and pamphlets, and attack people, sometimes beating them with *Bibles,* crosses, and clubs. The government of Georgia does not punish people who attack Jehovah's Witnesses.

Conscientious Objectors

Even in countries where it is legal for Jehovah's Witnesses to pray, have *Bible* study meetings, and witness door-to-door, Witnesses face challenges when they try to practice their beliefs related to citizenship. Children of Witnesses are often expelled from school for failing to salute the flag of their country. Adult male Witnesses are frequently jailed as conscientious objectors, people who, because of their personal beliefs, refuse to serve in the military.

Refusing to serve in the military does not lead to imprisonment in every country. Some countries, such as

Witnesses in Germany offer a prayer of thanks after a court ruled in 2005 that the German government must recognize Jehovah's Witnesses as an official religious body.

the United States, do not draft young men into their armed forces. In many countries, however, service in the military is required of all men whether the country is at war or not. In South Korea, where 90,000 Jehovah's Witnesses live, 1,000 Witnesses are currently in prison. There, conscientious objectors must serve an eighteen-month sentence. In Azerbaijan, the constitution states that conscientious objectors must be allowed to do an alternative peaceful service. However, because Azerbaijan does not yet have an alternative service set

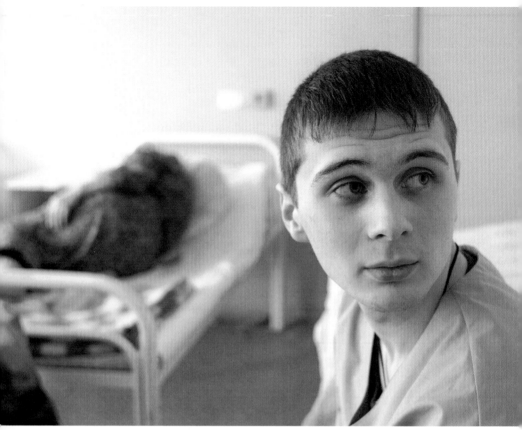

A Russian Jehovah's Witness awaits trial for refusing to serve in the military.

up for objectors, Azerbaijani courts have ruled that conscientious objectors must still be jailed. In Armenia, an alternative service exists, but many Witnesses consider it to be military service, because it is part of Armenia's defense department. Some still refuse to serve in it and are imprisoned. Those who do serve in Armenia's alternative service are often attacked and beaten for their beliefs by people who recognize the dark blue uniform of the alternative service.

As communities of Jehovah's Witnesses grow larger, governments of some countries begin to remove their freedom of religion, even if they were allowed to practice their faith peacefully in the past. In 1974, the country of Singapore responded to the refusal of some Jehovah's Witnesses to serve in the military by revoking the church registration of all its Witnesses, making their meetings illegal. Today, the 2,000 Witnesses living in Singapore are banned from carrying *Bibles* and *Watchtower*

Witnesses in Singapore like this man can be jailed for a year if they are caught carrying a bible.

literature. A Witness caught carrying a *Bible* in Singapore can be jailed for a year. In Eritrea, Witnesses lived peacefully until 1994, when Eritrea's president issued a decree stating that Witnesses had given up their rights as citizens by refusing to serve in the military. Following the decree, many Witnesses were fired from their jobs, stripped of their passports and other identity papers, and expelled from school. Eritrean police began raiding *Bible* study groups in private homes and arresting men, women, and children. In 2004, Witnesses ranging in age from 6 to 94 were imprisoned in Eritrean jails. In the same year, Rwandan Jehovah's Witnesses were arrested and beaten for refusing to participate in Rwanda's nighttime security patrols. Rwandan couples are beaten and jailed if they refuse to put their hands on the flag during their marriage ceremonies.

Court Battles

Despite the obstacles that they face in many parts of the world, Jehovah's Witnesses continue to witness door-to-door and to convert people. They have found a peaceful way to gain the right to practice their faith. They go to court to try to gain the freedom to practice their religion. For example, in Greece, Jehovah's Witnesses used to be regularly arrested for practicing a religion other than the state religion, Greek Orthodox (a denomination of Christianity). Greek Witnesses were arrested 19,147 times between 1938 and 1992. Finally, Witnesses took their case to the European Court of Human Rights. They won the case, securing the right to practice

In 2005 the European Court of Human Rights ruled that Witnesses had the right to freely practice their faith in the country of Greece.

their faith in Greece and in 40 other European countries.

In the United States, many states used to have laws requiring Jehovah's Witnesses to get a license to witness door-to-door and to assemble for meetings. Some even had laws requiring Witnesses to pay a fee, or to pay taxes, in order to be allowed to give away pamphlets and magazines. Many had laws requiring schools to expel children if they refused to salute the flag or say the Pledge of Allegiance. Jehovah's Witnesses challenged all of these laws in court. Between 1938 and 1955, they won 38 cases before the U.S. Supreme Court. These cases applied not just to Jehovah's Witnesses, but to all other religious groups in the United States as well.

Although Jehovah's Witnesses face persecution in many places around the world, they have managed to use peaceful methods to bring about changes. Many religious rights advocates use the way Jehovah's Witnesses are treated in a country as a measure of how much freedom of religion the people of that country have. When Jehovah's Witnesses have more freedom of religion, so, usually, do other religions. When a society begins to attack Jehovah's Witnesses, frequently other religions are in danger, too.

NOTES

Chapter One: How Did My Religion Begin?

1. Quoted in Watchtower Bible and Tract Society, *Jehovah's Witnesses in the Divine Purpose*. New York: Watchtower Bible and Tract Society, 1959, p. 377.

Chapter Two: What Do I Believe?

2. Quoted in Watchtower: Official Web site of Jehovah's Witnesses. www.watchtower.org.

GLOSSARY

Armageddon: God's war against Satan and evil, which will occur just before God's kingdom is established on Earth.

baptized: To immerse a believer in water to symbolize the beginning of that person's new life within a faith.

convert: To change to a different religion.

denomination: A branch of a religion.

disfellowshipping: Expelling a believer from the church on the grounds of immoral conduct or lack of faith.

end times: The last days before the war of Armageddon begins.

idolatry: Worshipping someone or something other than God.

kingdom of God: God's rule on Earth after the war of Armageddon has ended.

pray: To talk to God.

resurrected: Returned from the dead.

witness: To tell others about God and God's kingdom.

FOR FURTHER EXPLORATION

Books

Grant Wacker. *Religion in 19th Century America.* Oxford: Oxford University Press, 2000. Explains what the United States was like, and what issues American religious thinkers were particularly concerned about, at the time that Charles Taze Russell founded the Jehovah's Witnesses.

Watchtower Bible and Tract Society. *The New World Translation of the Holy Scriptures.* Pennsylvania: Watchtower Bible and Tract Society, 2004. The version of the *Bible* that Jehovah's witnesses use.

Web Sites

Bible Gateway (www.biblegateway.com). Includes a search engine that can be used to compare verses of the *Bible* from different translations. Useful for comparing versions of the *Bible* used by other denominations with the New World Translation used by Jehovah's Witnesses.

Christian Apologetics and Research Ministry (www.carm.org/witnesses.htm). A Web site maintained by Christian critics of Jehovah's Witnesses. Includes detailed discussions of Witness interpretations of different *Bible* verses.

Jehovah's Witnesses United (http://jehovah.to/index.htm). An unofficial Web site for Jehovah's Witnesses. The home page includes links to news reports about Jehovah's Witnesses and human rights around the world.

Office of Public Information of the Jehovah's Witnesses (www.jw-media.org/index.html). The official home page of the Jehovah's Witnesses Office of Public Information. Includes links to news reports about Jehovah's Witnesses, with sections on health and medicine, beliefs and practices, and human rights.

Watchtower: Official Web Site of Jehovah's Witnesses (www.watchtower.org). The official Jehovah's Witness Web site. Includes an online version of the New World Translation of the *Bible* and answers to frequently asked questions about Jehovah's Witnesses.

INDEX

PICTURE CREDITS

ABOUT THE AUTHOR

Marie Juettner is a writer and editor of children's reference books and educational videos. Originally from McGrath, Alaska, she currently lives in Kenosha, Wisconsin. This is her ninth book.